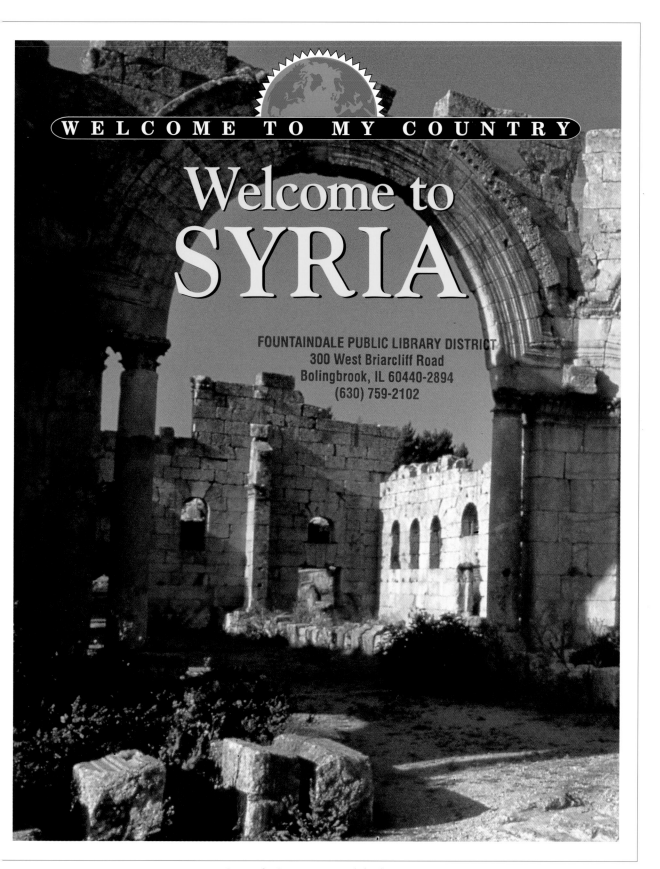

WELCOME TO MY COUNTRY

Welcome to
SYRIA

FOUNTAINDALE PUBLIC LIBRARY DISTRICT
300 West Briarcliff Road
Bolingbrook, IL 60440-2894
(630) 759-2102

Gareth Stevens Publishing
A WORLD ALMANAC EDUCATION GROUP COMPANY

Written by
ALAN TAY

Edited by
KATHARINE BROWN-CARPENTER

Edited in the U.S. by
JENETTE DONOVAN GUNTLY

Designed by
BENSON TAN

Picture research by
THOMAS KHOO
JOSHUA ANG

First published in North America in 2006 by
Gareth Stevens Publishing
A WRC Media Company
330 West Olive Street, Suite 100
Milwaukee, Wisconsin 53212 USA

Please visit our web site at
www.garethstevens.com
For a free color catalog describing
Gareth Stevens Publishing's list of high-quality
books and multimedia programs, call
1-800-542-2595 (USA) or 1-800-387-3178 (Canada)
Gareth Stevens Publishing's fax: (414) 332-3567.

© **MARSHALL CAVENDISH INTERNATIONAL (ASIA)**
PRIVATE LIMITED 2005
Originated and designed by
Times Editions—Marshall Cavendish
An imprint of Marshall Cavendish International (Asia) Pte Ltd
A member of Times Publishing Limited
Times Centre, 1 New Industrial Road
Singapore 536196
http://www.marshallcavendish.com/genref

Library of Congress Cataloging-in-Publication Data
Tay, Alan.
Welcome to Syria / Alan Tay.
p. cm. — (Welcome to my country)
Includes bibliographical references and index.
ISBN 0-8368-3136-5 (lib. bdg.)
1. Syria—Description and travel—Juvenile literature. I. Series.
DS94.T367   2005
956.91—dc22   2005042456

Printed in Singapore

1 2 3 4 5 6 7 8 9 09 08 07 06 05

PICTURE CREDITS
Agence France Presse: 15 (bottom), 16,
    17 (top), 19, 36 (both)
ANA Press Agency: 1, 6, 13, 14 (bottom),
    23, 29, 35 (top)
Art Directors & TRIP Photo Library: 2, 3 (top),
    5, 8, 10, 18, 27, 37, 38, 40, 41 (bottom)
Bes Stock: 9, 35 (bottom)
Focus Team Italy: 3 (middle & bottom), 21,
    22, 24, 25, 28, 33, 34, 41 (top), 43
HBL Photo Network: 14 (top)
Illustrated London News: 12
John R. Jones: 30, 31, 32, 45
Life File Photos: 7, 20, 26
North Wind Picture Archives: 11, 15 (top)
Still Pictures: 4
Travel Ink Photo & Feature Library: cover
Alison Wright: 39

Digital Scanning by Superskill Graphics Pte Ltd

Contents

Words that appear in the glossary are printed in **boldface** type the first time they occur in the text.

Welcome to Syria!

Syria is famous for its **ancient**, historic cities, such as Damascus and Palmyra. Since it became independent in 1946, Syria has fought many wars. Syria's government has also changed many times. These and other problems have kept Syria's economy from growing. Let's learn about Syria and its people!

Opposite: This picture was taken looking down on Damascus, which is Syria's capital city. Damascus is also the largest city in the country.

Below: The ancient city of Palmyra is famous around the world. It is located in central Syria.

The Flag of Syria

The red, white, and black bands on Syria's flag stand for freedom, peace, and the nation's **colonial** past. The two green, five-pointed stars in the middle of the white band stand for Syria and Egypt and Arab **independence**.

The Land

Syria has a land area of 71,479 square miles (185,180 square kilometers). This land area includes the Golan Heights, a region of land that Israel and Syria have fought over and Israel now rules. The Mediterranean Sea borders Syria on the west. Turkey, Iraq, Jordan, Israel, and Lebanon surround the rest of Syria.

Coastal plains cover a small area in western Syria. East of the plains is the Jabal an-Nusayriyah mountain range.

Below:
Rows of grapevines stretch across a valley. Vineyards can be found in the mountain valleys between Homs and Hamah, two cities in western Syria.

The Anti-Lebanon Mountains form the border between Syria and Lebanon. Syria's highest point, Mount Hermon, is in the Anti-Lebanon Mountains. It is 9,232 feet (2,814 meters) high. More than half of the nation is covered by the Syrian Desert. The desert is made up of sand desert and rock and gravel **steppe**.

Syria's largest rivers are the Orontes and the Euphrates. Large dams have been built on both rivers. The dams are used to produce **hydroelectric** power.

Above:
People walk across a bridge over the Euphrates River. The Euphrates is the most important source of water in Syria. It is also the only river in the country that can be traveled by boat.

Climate

Most of Syria is desert. The desert areas often get 5 inches (127 millimeters) of rain or less each year. The mountains and coast, however, get up to 40 inches (1,016 mm) of rain each year.

Syria's inland regions can get very hot. In Palmyra, summer temperatures can reach as high as 115° Fahrenheit (46° Celsius). In most regions, winter temperatures do not fall below freezing. On the coast, temperatures are usually about 50° F (10° C) or above. Rarely, snow or sleet may fall in inland regions.

Below:
Snow covers the mountains in the Golan Heights. During winter, it is often cold enough for snow to fall in the mountains of Syria. Most other areas of the country have mild winter temperatures.

Plants and Animals

Along Syria's coast, lemon and orange trees grow. In the mountains, shrubs and yew, fir, and lime trees grow. Few plants grow in Syria's desert regions.

Many animals live in Syria, including gazelles, hyenas, jackals, polecats, and badgers. Chameleons and lizards live in the desert. Buzzards, falcons, eagles, and many other birds also live in Syria.

Today, the growth of cities and the overuse of water have caused more of the land to become desert. To protect wildlife, Syria set up nature **reserves**.

History

The history of Syria dates back to about 3500 B.C. Syria was part of a larger area known as Greater Syria. It was ruled by the Egyptians, Babylonians, Hittites, Assyrians, Chaldeans, and Persians. In 333 B.C., Alexander the Great, who was from Macedonia, took control. The area later became part of the Roman **Empire** and then the Byzantine Empire. Arab **Muslims** took control in the 600s A.D.

Left:
These columns and arches stand in the city of Palmyra. They were built during Roman rule in the first century A.D. Palmyra grew under Roman rule and became an important center of trade. In 1089, the city was destroyed by an earthquake.

Left: This drawing shows the city of Antioch in Syria. For thousands of years, Antioch was an important stop along the Silk Road, a trade route that ran from Europe to East Asia. Today, Antioch is called Antikiya. It is now part of Turkey.

Ottoman Rule

In 1516, the Ottoman Turks took over Greater Syria. They ruled the area for four hundred years. To gain power in the Middle East, the British encouraged Arabs in the area to fight Ottoman rule. Sherif Hussein, who was the head of the Hashemite family, agreed to help lead the Arabs in the fight.

On June 5, 1916, Hussein's sons led a **revolt** against the Ottoman Turks. By October 1918, the fight was over, and the Arabs had won control. Hussein's son Faisal became the military governor of most of Syria. In 1919, the country declared its independence.

Short-Lived Arab Rule

The Arab revolt against the Ottomans happened during World War I. Sherif Hussein and the Arabs thought that the British promised them control of Syria. Six months after gaining Hussein's support, Britain gave Syria to France, one of the **Allies** in the war. In 1919, the Allies met to create a peace plan. Faisal attended. He wanted Syria to stay independent, but the Allies refused.

Below: Besides Syria, many other Arab states in the Middle East asked for independence during the 1919 Versailles Peace Conference in France. The Allies refused them all.

When Faisal returned to Damascus, he declared Syria independent anyway. In March 1920, the Syrians made Faisal king. Britain and France did not accept Syria's independence, however. French troops took over Damascus, ending all Arab control. Faisal fled the country.

A Nazi group ruled Syria for a short time during World War II. In 1941, free French and Arab forces took control of Syria again. In 1946, the nation became independent. In 1958, Syria and Egypt formed the United Arab **Republic**. In 1961, Syria became independent again.

Above: This picture shows a group of Arabs fighting the French. The French crushed the Arabs' fight for control when they marched into Damascus on July 25, 1920.

Modern Times

In November 1970, Hafez al-Assad led a violent takeover of Syria. He became president of Syria in March 1971 and ruled until his death in 2000.

While he was alive, Hafez al-Assad trained his son Bashar al-Assad to be Syria's next leader. After Hafez died, Bashar ran for president. No one ran against him, so Bashar was elected president of Syria on July 17, 2000.

Above: President Bashar al-Assad has used many Western methods to try to improve Syria's economy.

Left: Posters of Hafez al-Assad still hang all over Syria. In 1967, the Arab-Israeli war broke out. During fighting between Syria and Israel, Israel took control of the Golan Heights. During his time as president, Hafez worked to get the Golan Heights back. The fight for control of the area continues today.

Alexander the Great (356–323 B.C.)

In 333 B.C., Alexander the Great's army took over northern Syria. By 332 B.C., Alexander had taken full control of the region. He brought Greek architecture, art, and the Greek language to Syria.

Jamal Pasha (1872–1922)

Jamal Pasha, or Jamal the Butcher, was a military leader of the Ottoman army. He ordered the deaths of many Syrians who fought Ottoman rule.

Alexander the Great

Adib Shishakli (1909–1964)

Colonel Adib Shishakli tried to take over Syria's government in 1948 and 1951. In 1953, Shishakli was elected president. He ruled as a **dictator**. In 1954, he was forced to flee Syria.

Asma al-Assad

Asma al-Assad (1976–)

The wife of President Bashar al-Assad, Asma al-Assad has worked to improve life for Syrians. In 2001, she attended the first meeting of Arab first ladies.

Government and the Economy

The government of Syria has three branches. The president is the head of the executive branch and the armed forces. Bashar al-Assad was elected in 2000 for a seven-year term. He selected two vice presidents, a **prime minister**, and four deputy prime ministers, who assist the prime minister. He also chose a cabinet, or group of ministers.

Below:
Mustafa Tlass (*far right*) was sworn in as a member of Syria's cabinet by President Hafez al-Assad (*far left*) on March 20, 2000.

Left: On June 27, 2000, the People's Council met. They agreed that Bashar al-Assad could run for president. The council changed Syria's constitution to allow Bashar to run at the age of thirty-four instead of forty.

Syria's **legislative** branch consists of the People's Council. The council has 250 members. Members serve four-year terms and are elected by voters.

Syria's judicial branch includes civil and religious courts. The highest court is the Supreme **Constitutional** Court.

Since 1963, members of a political party called the Baath Party have ruled Syria's government. No one will run against the president, so the president holds almost total control. The Syrian people have little political power.

The Economy

Most Syrians used to work as farmers, mostly growing crops and raising cattle. Now, many Syrians work in industries, including the oil industry. Farming is still important in Syria, however. Crops grown in the nation include potatoes, cotton, wheat, olives, and lentils.

Many farmers have trouble growing crops today. Much of the land has been used too much, has been flooded, or has been watered too much. The problems have made it harder to grow plants.

Left: This woman is picking cotton by hand. In Syria, **traditional** farming methods are still used throughout the country.

Oil is one of Syria's most important natural resources. It is one of Syria's main **exports**. Other exports include fruits, vegetables, cotton, and products made from oil. The nation buys food, machinery, farm animals, metal, and metal products from other countries.

Besides oil, Syria has many other natural resources, such as natural gas, **phosphates**, and rock salt. Materials such as asphalt, gypsum, marble, iron, chrome, and manganese are also mined in the country.

People and Lifestyle

Today, almost all people living in Syria are Arabs. Some Armenians and Kurds also live in the country.

In the past, most people living in Syria belonged to **native** tribes. The tribes moved from place to place and mostly lived apart from other groups. Today, Syria has only a few native tribes. Syria's largest native tribe is the Ruwala. Other native tribes include the Hassana, the Butainat, and the Abadah.

Below: These Arabs are tending sheep outside the city of Hamah. Some Arabs in Syria still live in tribes that move from place to place.

Family Life

In Syria, families are at the center of life. A family's honor is based on how the family acts, especially the women. Most women in Syria wear modest clothes and do not have much contact with men who are not family members.

Syrian fathers are the heads of their households. Most fathers work outside the home. Most mothers stay home to care for their children and households. Children are taught a deep respect for their parents and elders.

Above: Family life is important to Syrians, and they usually spend their free time with family members. Syrian Muslims pray five times each day, so most activities are planned around prayer times.

Syrian Weddings

In Syria, marriages are often arranged. The groom's family asks the bride to marry him. The bride and groom sign a contract at a ceremony. They are then married, but they still live apart until a wedding is held a few weeks or months later. At the wedding, the bride and the groom sit with the women. The men sit apart. The couple cuts a cake and holds a gold ceremony. The groom gives his bride gold as part of the **bride-price**. A honeymoon often follows the wedding.

Above: This bride and groom are wearing traditional Syrian wedding clothes. Divorce is legal in Syria, but few Syrians are divorced.

Women in Syria

Recently, women in Syria were given the same legal rights that men have, but not everyone follows the laws. Some Syrian women in the countryside, for example, still cannot own property.

Most Syrian women still work at home, but some women are beginning to get jobs outside the home. Women are also beginning to hold important roles in society. In 2004, thirty women were members of the People's Council.

Below:
These women in Syria are working on a farm as onion pickers. In 1967, a group was set up to help women take more active roles in Syria's society.

Education

Children in Syria must attend primary school from age six to age twelve. The Arabic language is used to teach most classes. At age eight, Syrian students begin to learn a second language, such as English or French. After finishing primary school, students may attend lower secondary school. After three years, they take an exam to see whether they will take **vocational** or academic classes in upper secondary school.

Below: Children in Syria are supposed to attend school, but some girls in the countryside do not. Because of this, more boys than girls in Syria can read and write.

Left: Students in Syria must wear uniforms. In recent years, the number of Syrian students attending schools has gone up, so the nation has built new secondary schools and universities.

Higher Education

If students do well in upper secondary school, they may attend a university, a **technical** college, or another kind of school of higher learning. Syria's two main universities are Aleppo University and Damascus University. Programs of study at universities usually last four to six years. At most technical colleges, study programs last three years.

If they can afford to, many students in Syria choose to attend universities and colleges in other countries.

Religion

Almost all people in Syria are Muslims, and Islamic law is part of Syria's legal system. Like Muslims in many other countries, Syrian Muslims live by a set of religious rules called the Five Pillars of Islam. One of the rules is to recite a prayer called the *shahada* (shah-HAH-dah). The other rules are to pray five times a day, give money to the poor, make a **pilgrimage** to Mecca in Saudi Arabia, and fast during each day of Ramadan, the Islamic holy month.

Below: Like other Muslim men around the world, Muslim men in Syria visit mosques, or Islamic houses of worship, each Friday to pray. This mosque is in the city of Aleppo.

People who follow Islam belong to different Muslim groups. About three-fourths of Muslims in Syria are Sunni Muslims. Other Muslim groups in the country include the Shi'ites, Druzes, and Alawites.

Non-Muslim religions are present in Syria as well. Most non-Muslims in the country are Christian. Syrian Christians attend Roman Catholic, Orthodox, or Protestant churches. Fewer than one hundred Jews live in Syria. More Jews once lived in Syria, but many of them left to avoid harsh treatment by Arabs.

Above: These Syrian Christians are praying at the Deir Mar Moussa Monastery, which is a house for religious people. The people of Syria are free to choose their own religions.

Language

Arabic is the official language of Syria. Some Syrians also speak French. The French language was brought to Syria when France ruled the country. French is often spoken in cities and in business. Children in Syria must learn a second language in school, so most of them can speak either French or English.

Some Syrians speak other languages, such as Kurdish, Armenian, Aramaic, or Circassian.

Below: Although most street signs in Syria are written in Arabic, some signs, including these in the capital city of Damascus, contain English words.

Literature

In the past, Syria's literature included written poetry and poetry spoken out loud. Some Syrian writers became well known in the Middle East. Today, many Syrian writers are known for speaking out about politics and Syrian life. Some of the writers have been sent to prison for writing about the hardships and lack of freedom in Syria since the end of World War I. Two well-known Syrian writers are Hani al-Raheb (1939–2000) and Nihad Sirees (1950–).

Arts

Syria is famous for its beautiful crafts, including fabric weaving. The country is known for silk damask, a fabric that was first made in Damascus. Syria is also famous for gold brocade, which is fabric woven with gold thread. Some Syrian women are well known for their **embroidery**. It is sewn onto items such as gowns, jackets, and cushions. Trees and flowers are two popular patterns.

Left: This clothes shop is in a souk in Aleppo. A souk is a covered market that sells one kind of craft. This shop sells many of the embroidered items and fabrics that Syria has become famous for around the world.

Metalwork and Woodwork

Syria is known throughout the Middle East for its metalwork. Craft items are made from brass, copper, silver, and gold. Many kinds of metal items are made in Syria, including trays, boxes, and coffee pots with cups to match.

Woodwork intarsia is another famous Syrian craft. In this craft, small pieces of bone and mother-of-pearl, which is the shiny lining of a mollusk shell, are set into wood to make designs.

Art and Architecture

Syrians enjoy art. Today, Ikbal Karisly, Louai Kayyali, and May Abou Jeib are well-known Syrian artists.

Syria's past rulers created buildings in many different styles. These styles of architecture can still be seen in ancient cities such as Ebla and Aleppo. One of Syria's best examples of architecture is the Roman Theater, which was built in Bosra in the 100s A.D. Today, talented craftsmen travel all over Syria. They design and build many beautiful homes.

Below: This Syrian artist is holding a show of his work at the Artisan Center in Damascus. Art is important in Syria.

Singing and Dancing

Many Syrians like to sing and dance at family events. *Debke* (dib-KE) is one favorite traditional dance. People stand in a line to dance debke.

Theater

Theater in Syria is often used to speak out about political issues. The directors, actors, and play writers are known for risking their freedom in order to tell the audience about their views. One famous actor in Syria is Duraid Laham. In the 1970s, he was well known for his roles as victims of Syria's political system.

Leisure

Syrians spend most of their leisure time visiting with friends and family. Having a picnic or barbecue is a popular leisure activity. Often, families take *al manqal* (al MAN-kal), which are small grills, into the countryside to have barbecues.

Syrian families who have money to spare sometimes take vacations in other countries. Many families are very poor, however, and cannot afford vacations.

Below: In their free time, Syrian families often go on picnics. Because picnics are fun and do not cost a lot of money, even poor Syrian families can enjoy them.

Most Syrian men spend their leisure time at coffeehouses. Coffeehouses serve traditional coffee, Turkish coffee, Arabic tea, and many kinds of desserts.

Women do not go to coffeehouses. They visit other women at their homes to drink tea or coffee and enjoy dessert.

Syrian children spend most of their time at school or doing homework. If they have any free time, boys help their fathers with family businesses. Girls help their mothers with housework.

Above: Syrian men often meet at teahouses, such as this one in Tartus, to drink tea and talk.

Below: Some Syrian men enjoy smoking traditional water pipes.

Sports

Syria's most popular sport is soccer. Syrians attend soccer games and watch soccer on television. Many children in Syria play soccer in the streets. Another favorite sport in Syria is basketball.

Syrians have competed in worldwide sporting events. Syria also has hosted events such as the Pan-Arab Games. At the 1996 Olympics, Ghada Shouaa won the heptathlon, a contest for women that consists of seven track-and-field events.

Above:
Ghada Shouaa is a well-known Syrian athlete. Here, she is celebrating after winning the gold medal in the high jump event at the Pan-Arab Games held in 1999.

Left: The national soccer team of Syria poses for a picture before its game against the Philippines in 2001. The game was held in Aleppo. The two teams played to win a place in the 2002 World Cup, which is the world's top soccer competition.

Left: Pure Arabian horses are listed in the Syrian Arab Horse Stud Book. Some Bedouins in Syria do not list their horses because they are afraid the government will take them.

Arabian Horses

Bedouins, native Arab tribes in Syria and other countries, were the first to breed and race Arabian horses. In Syria today, breeding and racing Asil Arabian horses is still popular. In July 1990, the government of Syria began publishing the Syrian Arab Horse Stud Book. The book keeps track of the pure Arabian horses born in Syria. It includes details about the many families of horses in the country. Today, there are more than one thousand pure Arabian horses in Syria.

National Holidays

Many national holidays are celebrated in Syria. The first holiday of the year is New Year's Day on January 1. March 8 is Revolution Day. It honors the day in 1963 when the Baath Party took power. **Martyrs'** Day is May 6. On that day in 1915, Arabs from a group called the Al Fatat were arrested. Many were killed. Independence Day, on April 17, marks the day in 1946 when French control of Syria ended. Syrians also celebrate holidays such as Mother's Day on March 21 and Labor Day on May 1.

Left: These flags celebrate the *hajj* (HAJ), which is the annual pilgrimage that Muslims make to Mecca in Saudi Arabia. Like these flags, decorations for Muslim holidays often are covered in Arabic writing.

Religious Holidays

For Syria's Muslims, Ramadan is the most important holiday of the year. It is the ninth month of the Islamic calendar. During Ramadan, Muslims do not eat or drink from dawn to dusk. Ramadan ends with a three-day feast called *Eid al-Fitr* (EED al-FIT-er). *Eid al-Adha* (EED al-AD-ha), or the Feast of the **Sacrifice**, follows the hajj period.

Syrian Christians celebrate religious holidays such as Easter and Christmas. Christmas in Syria is kept very simple.

Above:
Muslim women gather at a mosque in Damascus. Each evening during the month of Ramadan, most Muslim men go to mosques to pray. Women may choose to pray at a mosque or at home.

Food

Food in Syria is flavorful and usually includes spices such as cloves, nutmeg, and cinnamon. The *mezze* (me-ZIH) is popular in Syria. It is more than forty small dishes served together with bread. It may include hummus, a paste made of chickpeas, or *baba ghanoush* (BA-ba ga-NOOJ), which is baked eggplant. A main dish of lamb, fish, or chicken is usually served after the mezze.

Below: Different types of nuts and dried fruits are often used in Syrian cooking. They are also delicious to eat on their own.

Left: Many fruit shops in Syria sell fruits, such as figs, oranges, apricots, grapefruits, pears, apples, and plums, that were grown in the nation.

Most Syrian meals include olive oil, bread, and dairy foods such as white cheese. Many Syrians also eat *bulgar* (BUL-gah), which is boiled, dried, and crushed wheat. It is rolled into balls and filled with meat, onions, and nuts.

At mealtime, the main food is usually served in one large dish. Most often, it is meat and rice served with side dishes such as salad and yogurt. If guests come for a meal in Syria, the men and women eat in separate areas.

Below: The kind of bread Syrians eat most often is called pita bread in the West. Syrians tear off a piece of the bread and use it like a scoop to pick up food.

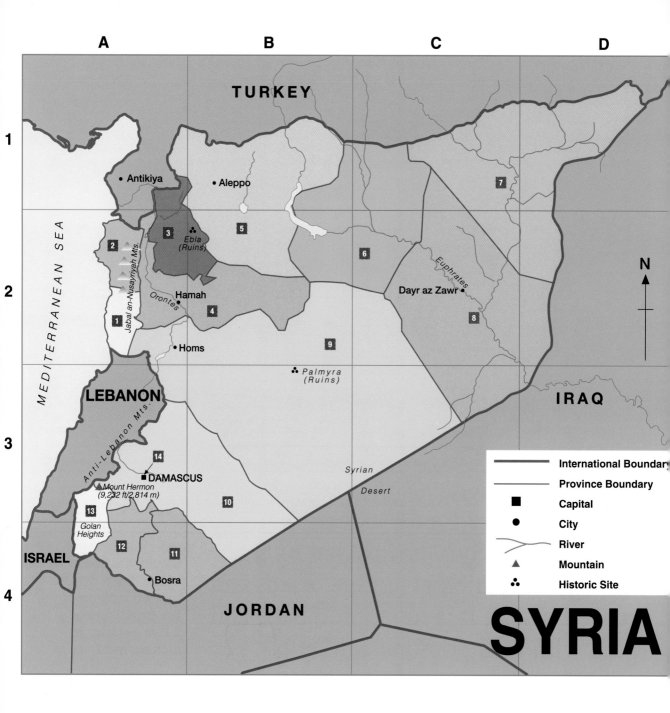

Provinces

1 Tartus	**5** Halab	**9** Homs	**13** Al-Qunaytirah
2 Al-Ladhiqiyah	**6** Ar Raqqah	**10** Dimashq	**14** Rif Dimashq
3 Idlib	**7** Al-Hasakah	**11** As Suwayda'	
4 Hamah	**8** Dayr az Zawr	**12** Dar'a	

Above: Beautiful paintings cover the outside of the Omayyad Mosque in Damascus.

Aleppo B1
Antikiya (Antioch) A1
Anti-Lebanon
    Mountains A3

Bosra A4

Damascus A3

Ebla B2
Euphrates River
    B1–D3

Golan Heights A3–A4

Hamah A2
Homs A2

Iraq C3–D4
Israel A3–A4

Jabal an-Nusayriyah
    Mountains A2
Jordan A4–C4

Lebanon A2–A3

Mediterranean Sea
    A1–A4
Mount Hermon A3

Orontes River
    A2–A3

Palmyra B3

Syrian Desert
    B3–C3

Turkey A1–D1

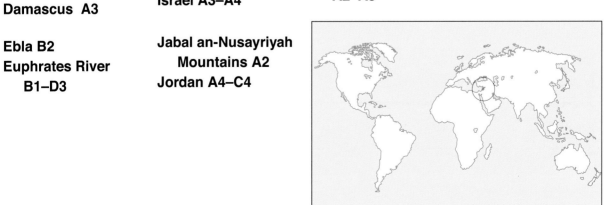

Quick Facts

Official Name Syrian Arab Republic

Capital Damascus

Official Language Arabic

Population 18,016,874 (July 2004 estimate)

Land area 71,479 square miles (185,180 square kilometers)

Provinces Al-Hasakah, Al-Ladhiqiyah, Al-Qunaytirah, Ar Raqqah, As Suwayda', Dar'a, Dayr az Zawr, Dimashq, Halab, Hamah, Homs, Idlib, Rif Dimashq, Tartus

Highest Point Mount Hermon 9,232 feet (2,814 meters)

Border Countries Iraq, Israel, Jordan, Lebanon, Turkey

Major Rivers Euphrates, Orontes

Main Religions Islam, Christianity

Holidays New Year's Day (January 1), Revolution Day (March 8), Mother's Day (March 21), Independence Day (April 17), Labor Day (May 1), Martyrs' Day (May 6), Christmas (December 25)

Currency Syrian Pound (50.02 SYP = US $1 as of 2004)

Opposite: The Great Mosque in the city of Aleppo can be seen through this doorway.

45

Glossary

Allies: a group of countries during World War I that worked together to fight Germany and Austria-Hungary.

ancient: relating to being very old.

bride-price: a payment given to the family of the bride by the groom or the groom's family.

colonial: regarding a settlement in one nation that is ruled by another nation.

constitutional: regarding a nation's set of laws, including citizen rights.

dictator: a ruler who keeps complete control of a country, often by force.

embroidery: the art of decorating cloth or clothes with fancy sewing.

empire: a very large collection of lands or regions ruled by one group.

exports (n): products sent out of a country to be sold in another country.

hydroelectric: regarding electricity that is made when water passes through a dam and into a river below.

independence: being free from the control of others.

legislative: relating to lawmaking.

martyrs: people who die or suffer rather than give up their religions or beliefs.

Muslims: people who belong to the religion of Islam.

native: belonging to a land or region by having first grown or been born there.

phosphates: acids that can be used in items such as drinks and fertilizers.

pilgrimage: a journey made to a holy place as an act of religious devotion.

prime minister: the highest adviser in a country's government, usually under a ruler or president.

republic: a country in which citizens elect their own lawmakers.

reserves: lands set aside so that animals and plants can survive there.

revolt: a fight against the government, often involving violence.

sacrifice: an offering of a valuable thing, often animals or people, to a god.

steppe: a large area of dry, flat land that does not have any trees.

technical: relating to using machines or science to perform a job or task.

traditional: regarding customs or styles passed down through the generations.

vocational: relating to a job, profession, or skilled trade.

More Books to Read

Ancient Euphrates. Geography of the World series. Charnan Simon (Child's World)

Arabian Horses. Animal Kingdom series. Julie Murrary (Budy Books)

Bedouin of the Middle East. First Peoples series. Elizabeth Losleben (Lerner Publishing)

I Am Muslim. Religions of the World series. Jessica Chalfonte (Powerkids Press)

Muslim Mosque. Places of Worship series. Angela Wood (Gareth Stevens)

The Ottoman Empire. Life during the Great Civilizations series. Lucille Davis (Blackbirch Press)

Peregrine Falcon. Animals under Threat series. Mike Unwin (Heinemann)

Ramadan. On My Own Holidays series. Susan Douglass (Lerner Publishing)

Syria. Fiesta! series. (Grolier)

Videos

The Middle East: Syria, Jordan, and Lebanon. (Lonely Planet)

Ramadan. Holidays for Children video series. (Schlessinger)

Web Sites

plasma.nationalgeographic.com/ mapmachine/profiles/sy.html

www.factmonster.com/ipka/ A0108016.html

www.plumsite.com/arabic/index.html

www.syriatourism.org/new/

Due to the dynamic nature of the Internet, some web sites stay current longer than others. To find additional web sites, use a reliable search engine with one or more of the following keywords to help you locate information about Syria. Keywords: *Aleppo, Damascus, Euphrates, Golan Heights, Mount Hermon, Palmyra.*

Index